I0173208

BOUNTY NOW AND FOREVER

BOUNTY NOW AND FOREVER
VITALITY OF FORMATION

a parent's guide to Catholic Catechism

Kathleen Bennett

Haley's
Athol, Massachusetts

© 2019 by Kathleen Bennett

All rights reserved. With the exception of short excerpts in a review or critical article, no part of this book may be re-produced by any means, including information storage and retrieval or photocopying equipment, without written permission of the publisher, Haley's.

Haley's
488 South Main Street
Athol, MA 01331
haley.antique@verizon.net
978.249.9400

International Standard Book Number: 978-1-948380-13-3

Copy edited by Christine Schroeder.
Proof read by Richard Bruno.

Images, including cover image by ifong,
purchased from Pexels.com and Shutterstock.com

Biblical verses from
New Revised Standard Version, Catholic Gift Edition

Information in *Bounty Now and Forever* supplied by
Breaking Bread with Daily Mass Propers,
    Oregon Catholic Press
33 Days to Morning Glory,
    Marian Press
Symbolon DVD series,
    Augustine Institute

for my grandchildren
Kaylie, Alexa, and Nikolas
and to
children and grandchildren everywhere

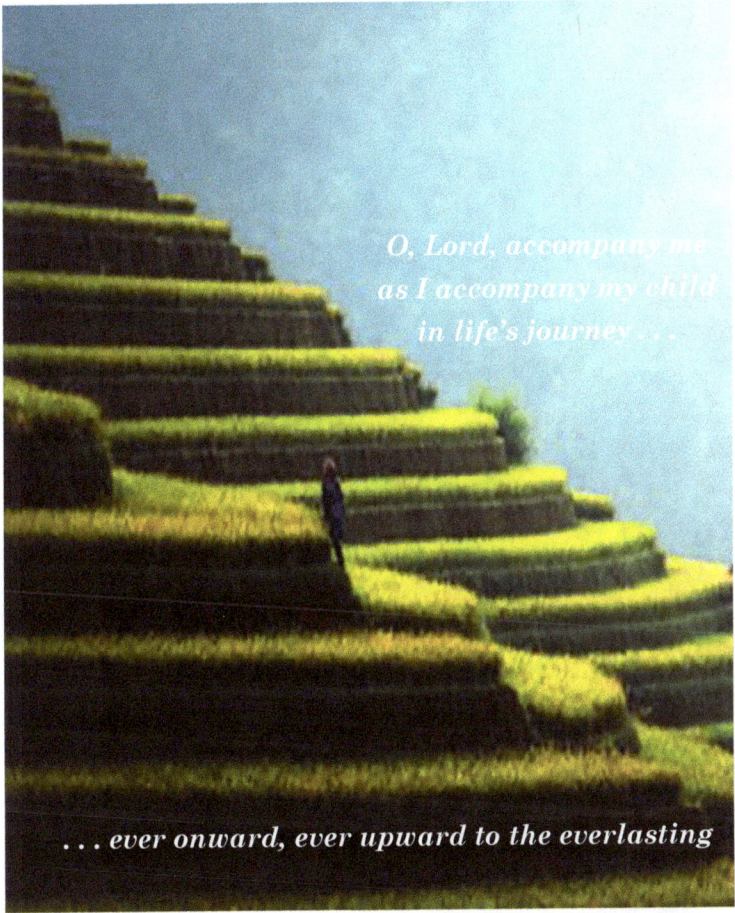

*O, Lord, accompany me
as I accompany my child
in life's journey . . .*

. . . ever onward, ever upward to the everlasting

public domain photo courtesy of Pexels.com

Contents

Contents

Desire to Provide a Sound and Firm Faith Foundation

a foreword by Father Patrick Ssekyole
pastor, Holy Cross Parish and Saint Martin Mission
Templeton, Massachusetts

I deeply thank Kathleen Bennett for the idea of and actual writing of *Bounty Now and Forever,* a quick-to-read book aimed at helping parents of our faith community to engage actively in the ministry of forming and educating our children in some fundamentals or basics of our Catholic faith. The content of *Bounty Now and Forever* indicates the depth of her desire to provide a sound and firm faith foundation to the youngsters of our faith community so that they can conduct their lives, confront challenges of our day-to-day lives, and confidently answer questions that will inevitably come their way, either directly or cunningly, regarding the relevance of being a faithful Catholic Christian in today's world.

Dear Parent, please reflectively read the content of *Bounty Now and Forever* chapter by chapter and allow it to move you to participate actively in the faith formation and education of our faith community, starting with your own child or children, for the greater glory of God through the continued growth of His Church on earth.

Desire to Provide a Sound and Firm Faith Foundation

The Fullness of Our Faith

Is the path to religious formation an easy one? Surely, it is not! And we need to be vigilant about what we or our children consume in that area of our lives. These times are challenging, to be certain. Conveying to school-aged children the goodness of God and all that is sacred somehow often doesn't seem to fit in today's lifestyles.

It takes special energy to hold steadfast in the twenty-first-century electronic age. Do not be afraid, though. All that we learned growing up in the catechism of our beloved Roman Catholic Church, even if our faith is or was as small as a mustard seed, is all we need now. It helps us safeguard against religious indoctrination as we come to understand the inseparability of faith and reason. *Faith* enlightens *reason*, and *reason* clarifies *faith*.

Our Catholic—from the Greek katholikos or univer-sal—Church is the universal Christian Church formed in Jesus's time by Jesus himself. We possess a two-thousand year-history traced all the way back to the Apostles, all of whom gave their lives for the advance of the Gospel, or *Good News*.

Following Christ's Ascension, when his disciples received the gift of the Holy Spirit, the spreading of

Jesus's teaching *lit the world on fire.* Consider that our world's measure of time itself became rearranged according to Before Christ and Anno Domini, Latin for In the Year of The Lord, which commenced after the world-changing event of the Resurrection of our Lord, Jesus Christ.

Our Catholicism is firmly centered on the Blessed Trinity, a barely comprehensible but awesome mystery. There's a wealth of strength in the power of our Almighty Father, redemption from our shortcomings through our Savior, Jesus Christ, and the enlightenment and consolation of the Holy Spirit.

Thus, the faith that the Catholic Church teaches, or hands down, traces back to the very time of Creation. Ours is a faith rooted in the First and Second Covenants that God has made with humanity. The faithful honor and cherish the seamless revelation of the God of the Old Testament and the New Testament. The God who was, who is, and who will be . . . the God who has no beginning and has no end: the God of the entire created order . . .

Four Anchoring Elements of the Roman Catholic Church

As we delve into anchoring elements, let us keep in mind the four marks of the Church that we repeat often in the Nicene Creed that the Church is: One, Holy, Catholic, and Apostolic.

✝ Magisterium

So what Christ has ordained for genuine discipleship, guidance in true faith, and unity in worship culminates through headship. Beginning with Simon Peter, whom Jesus renames Peter, meaning rock, Jesus tells his apostles that upon the Rock, that is, Peter, his Church shall be built. Such headship, crucial for a church on fire to the ends of the earth, is officially called Magisterium, in other words, the teaching authority of the Church. Magisterium throughout the ages—from the very first headship to the present day—leads the Church through the office of the papacy.

Our pope, the successor to Peter, has the massive task of strengthening us in the faith and overseeing Christ's entire Church (Luke 22:31-32). In order to accomplish that magisterial task, the pope works with the bishops, successors of the apostles, to ensure an authentic handing on of the Faith over all the earth. The Church requires such organization in the passing down of God's anointing of priests and deacons for the salvation of souls.

In addition to the immense responsibility of governing the worldwide Church to remain in unity, the Magisterium completed the gargantuan and sacred task of gathering all biblical scrolls and the apostles' pastoral epistles as well as transcribing and preserving them. Built on the cornerstone of Jesus, who fulfilled the Law and the Prophets of the

Old Testament, many writings of the books of the New Testament go back to the first century AD.

✝ Scripture

Through the centuries, we are beneficiaries of that catalog of Sacred Scripture, the revelation of God's Old and New Covenants, or Testaments. Theologians and clergy study both testaments intensely. We, the laity, too, may draw great spiritual food from our own reading of the Holy Bible, in addition to hearing parts of it in the Liturgy during Mass.

✝ Sacraments

Keeping in Jesus's example and instruction is the implementation of Sacraments. The Sacraments bless every aspect of our human lives from the first days of our birth until our last days on earth. As much as other demands of our earthly living take us in all directions, the Sacraments keep us connected to our Lord's perfect plan for our salvation through his life, death, and resurrection. We remain grounded in God's love when we receive the blessings of the Sacraments in the process of our sanctification.

Jesus tells us, "Abide in me as I abide in you. Just as the branch cannot bear fruit by itself unless it abides on the vine, neither can you unless you abide in me." (John 15:4) The Sacraments help us in our effort and process of abiding in Jesus Christ and bearing fruit.

It is our heritage to reel in the Sacraments, living our lives as heirs to such glorious inheritance and passing down such richness to our children. You are indeed continuing that very important aspect of your children's spiritual dimension.

☦ Traditions

Traditions serve as the rhythm of our worship. They help us remain in touch with the history of the handing down of our faith. Coming together as a community— think common unity—by celebrating the Mass weekly keeps our souls and inner spirits nourished. The Liturgy, through its Liturgical seasons of Advent, Christmas, Lent, Easter, and Ordinary Times, holds us steadfast in communion with our Maker and Redeemer.

Traditional sacramentals comprise gentle reminders of the sacred and edifying presence of God. During certain inevitable trials, a man, a woman, or a child may draw strength at a particular moment from the presence of sacramentals. Sacramentals such as statues, holy water, rosary beads, a cross, a crucifix, or even a well-read Holy Bible prompt us to contemplate God's call in our lives. Often, in our times of tribulation, they may comfort us with just our gaze upon them. Though Catholics believe in what is unseen in the form of spirit, sacramentals aid our minds to call upon the Trinity in some way every time we use them or gaze upon them.

As we regard our traditions with holiness and make them fundamental in our daily living, we shall indeed render our spirits eternally blessed.

Christian faith requires more than background information. Practicing faith retains a righteous relationship with God and blossoms throughout our lives because we are called to be active participants in our salvation. Living in faith takes constant nurturing and discernment of God's call to holiness, putting into practice the knowledge of our Faith.

So what exactly do we mean by faith?

Faith is . . . Trust. So, trusting in God's *Love*, God's *Omnipotence*, God's *Omnipresence*, his *Mercy*, and his *Faithfulness to all generations* remains paramount. Knowing that we can come to him with anything and everything ultimately soothes the soul. In his Truth and Love, we thrive.

Embracing all the tools that our Catholic Church has given us, including Sacraments, Holy Scripture, and Traditions—under the direction of the Magisterium reaps absolute blessings of peace, joy, love, and salvation.

Being, or becoming, closer to our Creator through communion with him in prayer in our everyday, busy lives is what separates us from a dark and destructive secularism that sweeps current-day society. Such godlessness deprives souls of joy, peace, pure love, and the hope that our faith engenders.

May we be reminded that God created us in his own likeness and therefore with the capacity to know right from wrong, good from bad, and to love and to be loved. Let us never forget that God created us in his own likeness, even among all the imperfections in our own lives with their challenges, especially in our harried world.

It has been quite a long time since each one of us has gone through the CCD program. From one generation to the next, CCD serves our youth by aiding them in forming moral consciences and in understanding God and his goodness more fully in regard to a relationship with him and with others, which is of utmost importance in a child's formative years.

Perhaps many of us as young children may not have entirely comprehended or fully appreciated our catechism during our childhoods. Often, due to life experiences, one fathoms a good catechism well only after one's graduation from such teaching.

Let us not forget the subtlety of spiritual growth, and let us not be afraid to persevere. In the Book of Galatians, Saint Paul expresses the idea well.

So let us not grow weary in doing what is right, for we will reap at harvest time if we do not give up.
—Galatians 6:9

We possess a propensity for our intellects to learn. In knowledge, we possess all the more to embrace. You, together with our CCD staff, can pass on the knowledge, values, and beauty of all that our beloved Catholic religion has to offer to our precious next generation.

Please know that in your faith community, the pastor, religious education coordinator, CCD teachers, and religious education board are here to help you every step of the way. If ever you have any questions, concerns, or suggestions, or if you wish to become more involved, such as by volunteering as a CCD teacher or joining the religious education board, please feel free to contact any one of us. We are here to love and to serve God joyfully in our capacities within his Church and our parish.

May God bless you and your families, and the whole of our Church community.

First Fruits of Our Time

How does one make time for daily prayer and reflection, which are necessary for a relationship with God?

One way is by giving thanks to God with every meal. As surely as we need food every single day—several times a day, we can and should take a moment to say a mealtime prayer, such as Grace.

What if our breakfasts or our dinners are hurried or not taken together as a family? The simple act of bowing our heads as we sit down to eat a meal individually is an easy ritual to constitute. For just a moment, do not think of that first bite without thanking God for his providence of the abundance he blesses us to have. We make brief acknowledgement, but the act of giving thanks to God regularly, with sincerity, means much in gratitude.

Saying Grace around the dinner table with our entire household has a powerful impact on our children, more than we may realize. The unity in prayer, gratitude, and acknowledgment that all things come from God reminds us of those blessings. A childhood steeped in such ritual stays with children for a lifetime.

Reciting in unison from the heart, "Bless us, O Lord, and these thy gifts which we are about to receive, from thy bounty, through Christ, Our Lord. Amen," may be the very first inkling a young child experiences that God exists and is much greater than any of us, individually and collectively.

How else may we fit more time into our busy lives—for communing with God?

You are parents of young children and you have homes to maintain. You may have fulltime jobs outside the home. Your children may be involved in one or more extracurricular activities throughout the year. Myriad other matters occupy time or deplete energy on any given day. How do we manage? Where do we get our strength?

At the end of a typical day, bodies tired and brains frazzled, we may feel anxiety at the thought of the next day that renders us limp and numb by evening. The kids may bicker with each other or with us; they need something tended to that we may or may not deem urgent enough to handle in the moment. Maybe we've had a bad day ourselves. Who has time or energy before we drop into bed to pray to God? Who cares about anything at that point?

The gift of time awaits us before our day begins. What will it take for us to carve out quality quiet time as we awaken fresh from slumber? For those who already do that, the sacrifice of a slightly earlier wake time—or rearranging routines—inarguably reaps benefits. Unless you care for an infant or toddler whose needs you must meet first, you will find it entirely possible to set aside time. Giving the first fruits of each day to God sets the tone of the entire day. How?

> *Be still and know that I am God.*
> —Psalm 46:10

The quietness of early morning likely offers the best time to give yourself over to a deeper relationship with God. Find a comfortable chair and sit down; perhaps settle down with a nice mug of coffee. The mind has not yet wound up; the body, still not quite ready for motion. Appliances and gadgets that we so heavily rely on remain in sleep-mode as well. Keep them there for a short while.

To be in communion with God is to be in conversation with God. Sometimes we may not know what to say or even how to begin. Be still, for God may speak to you. How else could we ever hear amid all the clutter of our minds?

In addition to conversing directly with God, as in prayer, other ways can draw us to God. Daily devotionals, reading scripture or other Catholic works, or writing in a spiritual journal are just some of the other ways that we may spend the first fruits of our time alone with the Lord.

Prayer

The act of praying pleases God. Do we pray because God needs to hear our praise and our petitions or requests?

> *Even before a word is on my tongue, O Lord, you know it completely.*

—Psalm 139:4

The act of praying pleases God.

11

No, God does not need us. We need him.

Yes, he loves us, but it is we who need him. He knows already what is on our minds and in our hearts. Our blinders fall away and true openness allows God's light to penetrate the eye only when we come to the realization that communion with God through prayer has more to do with our relating back to him heart to heart.

Internal prayer comprises the only way we converse with our God, both in good moments and in bad moments. Through prayer, we show God that we do not merely wait for him to give us good things and come to our help. We also depend on his helping us in everything, especially when we don't know what to ask or how to ask—but with prayer, nevertheless.

God's good pleasure includes that we open up to him. To our father, Abba (a familial term, like Daddy), we can bring up anything at all. We experience a searching in the soul, even in the darkest corners, propelling our very necessary baby steps leading toward the healing, guidance, and consolation of the Holy Spirit. Prayer reaps so many blessings if only we lay bare our inmost thoughts that otherwise we gloss over or escape from in the course of a day.

Communication with God involves a two-way connection with the soul. Allowing that connection, for some, may feel apprehensible, but fear not. By making room for sitting quietly with eyes shut and a deep exhale, one may very well find a prompting with utmost clarity that gently speaks intimately to oneself. We can come to God as we would to our best confidant, because the

Holy Spirit of God is our best confidant. God knows what we need, and even though the end result may not be exactly what we prayed for, rest assured, in God's time, he answers our prayers in even greater and more unexpected ways if we keep the faith.

While prayed requests may feel unanswered or as if sitting in some sort of queue in an angel's cubicle in heaven, God has many workings going on behind the scenes. Think of morning quiet time in prayer not as languishing in limbo but rather as time to rest in God's care while knowing that a greater blessing awaits. Through existing or even further trials and tribulations, children as well as adults find time to reflect and grow in virtues.

So much reveals itself to us as we indulge in God's Word. We should be amazed at the workings of our God! The Book of Hebrews summarizes the idea concisely when Saint Paul tells us,

> *So do not throw away your confidence: it will be richly rewarded.*

—Hebrews 10:35

Humility

From an early age, we may have fallen into the habit of praying only at times when we really want something or when a challenging situation arises or gets worse. Naturally, such moments feel important to us. God cares about them, too. What we should always take into consideration: Whom should we consider the natural (created), and whom should we consider the supernatural (creator)? Who should we consider central to whom in the supernaturally ordered realm? Does the sun revolve around earth? Or does earth revolve around the sun?

If the sun were to revolve around the earth, that would be greatly disordered. Chaos would ensue. The law of gravity plus the intense heat would surely lead to earth's swift demise. Rather, the creator has designed us creatures to revolve around the sun. In the spiritual sense, the Son, Jesus Christ, exists as central to our lives.

In other words, because God is the Almighty Creator, we must humbly approach him.

> For as the heavens are higher than the earth, so are my ways higher than your ways, and my thoughts than your thoughts.
>
> —Isaiah 55:9

Meaningful components to relational prayer begin with the Sign of the Cross, which invokes the Father in our minds, the Son in our hearts, and the Holy Spirit in our very beings. The full substance of our openness in communicating to our Lord includes praise, thanksgiving, contrition, and petition. Most of all, faith underlines meaningful praying to God, even in our periods of weakness and doubt—especially in our moments of weakness and doubt.

Bring it all to God.

> The Lord is near to the brokenhearted and saves the crushed in spirit. Many are the afflictions of the righteous, but the Lord rescues them from them all.
>
> —Psalm 34:19-20

We praise God in humility. Children should have a concept of humility and honor from an early age by the mere fact that we teach them to honor their father and mother. Even as adults, we should apply that precept to the glory and honor of our Father in heaven.

Giving thanks, even if our pressing needs seem to push thanksgiving behind them, should precede our petitions.

Rejoice always, pray without ceasing, give thanks in all circumstances, for this is the will of God in Christ Jesus for you.
—1Thessalonians 5:16-18

When we approach God in humility, we then realize how far we may have fallen from God's glory in our thoughts and in our deeds. We find it hard to say the word sin. The thought that we sin unsettles us. Often, we deny the fact that we may have done something (or not have done something) or said something demonstrating our poor behavior. It hurts our pride perhaps more than the hurt we feel we may have caused another human being: perhaps the end result of the subtle grip of relativism, which erodes our Christian value system. We should not adopt an amoral mindset that denies the existence of sin if we choose to think, for example, that if God does not exist, sin does not exist. We should not give in to such distorted reasoning, even if it seems to be a prevalent outlook.

We must guard against such distortion.

To the pure all things are pure, but to the corrupt and unbelieving nothing is pure. Their very minds and consciences are corrupted. They profess to know God, but they deny him by their actions.
—Titus 1:15-16

We should do the right thing and acknowledge our wrongdoing. We should pray for forgiveness. Shouldn't we always aim to resist the near occasion of sin?

No testing has overtaken you that is not common to everyone. God is faithful, and he will not let you be tested beyond your strength, but with the testing he will also provide the way out so that you may be able to endure it.
—1Corinthians 10:13

In such earnestness, we rely on our faith of great strength. If our faith sometimes weakens, we can simply give that over to God, too. Praying for increased faith perhaps could and should be our first petition. We could request God's special grace for our inner faith.

We do the most effective thing by demonstrating to our children the practice of praying.

Whether praying together as a family or sitting on our child's bed at night to encourage and listen to his or her prayers, we can emphasize keeping the line of communication between God and ourselves open. Once we open our hearts, we definitively draw strength. We do not have to carry burdens on our own of any kind. We would short-change our children by not fostering prayer to Abba. Youngsters need the 'confidant' that begets the precious gift of inner strength to accompany them throughout their lives.

Getting to know our Lord—and our desire to keep gravitating toward his love, mercy, and hope—transforms and refines the very best in us. As much as they need food and water, our children also possess an innate need for inner sanctum—a place where they can communicate with and trust in God—in order to flourish.

Sometimes, the best way to grow involves getting down on our knees to do necessary weeding—decluttering our minds and our days. We can never start the ritual of communication with God too early, and it is also never too late, but let us never procrastinate with prayer.

Do not worry about anything, but in everything by prayer and supplication with thanksgiving let your requests be made known to God. And the peace of God, which surpasses all understanding, will guard your hearts and your minds in Christ Jesus.

—Philippians 4:6-7

The Holy Bible

Reading scripture on our own reveals a world of wealth in our palms or on our screens. Owning a Catholic Bible provides a great resource—one of the best tools we can invest in and take to heart in our own homes. If, in our quiet time with the Lord, words don't come to us, reaching for Holy Scripture to read serves as prayer.

Immersing ourselves in the Word of God equates to hearing God. Christians grow in knowledge and

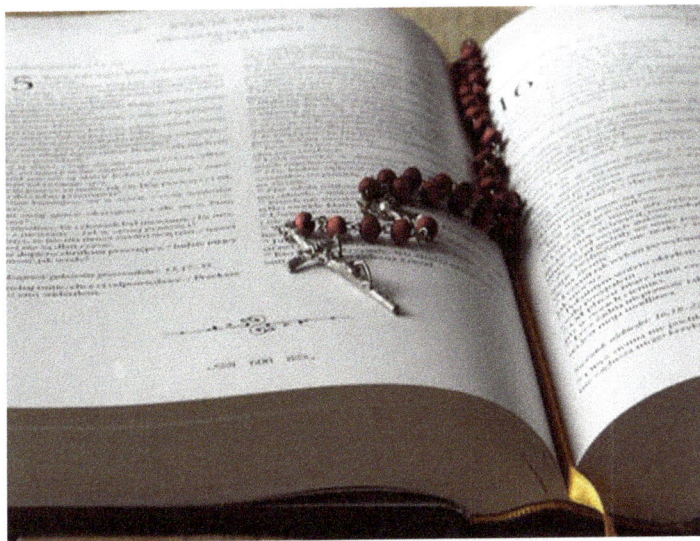

Owning a Catholic Bible provides a great resource.

public domain photo courtesy of Pexels.com

immeasurable blessings while forming an understanding of all that God is—and our relationship with God, with others, and even with our planet earth.

Scripture opens but a glimpse of God's infinite wisdom and sovereignty. Reading God's Word doesn't substitute for hearing the readings and gospel message at Sunday Mass. Still, scripture or other affirming Catholic books serve as a bridge—a nutritious snack, if you will—between moments of receiving the Mass's Living Bread.

Involvement

The preciousness of life begins an awesome journey. Do you remember marveling at what you and your mate procreated as you fell in love at first sight of your newborn? Oh, if only we could remain basking in such wonder!

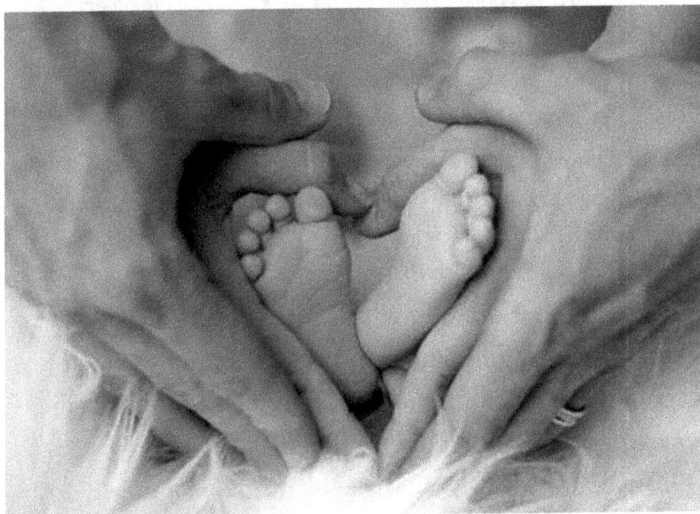

public domain photo courtesy of Pexels.com

Do you remember marveling at what you and your mate procreated as you fell in love at first sight of your newborn?

But soon enough, responsibilities of caring and providing for our growing families inevitably overwhelm preoccupied minds.

We've made arrangements to baptize our newborn. It is what our parents did for us, and our baby deserves no less.

What happens after the glow of the Sacrament of Baptism? Just as we feed and protect the physically growing child, so, too, we must nurture the seed-and-soil within our child's youthful heart and soul. Our child warrants no less throughout all the critical, formative years. It is right and good to register our child in religious formation, a/k/a CCD. There is so much to learn, so much to understand about our eternal and almighty, loving and just God and his plan for us, especially in our angst-filled times.

> *Know that the Lord is God. It is he that made us, and we are his; we are his people, and the sheep of his pasture. For the Lord is good; his steadfast love endures forever, and his faithfulness to all generations.*

—Psalm 100:3-5

There is a constancy of spiritual cultivating to do.

> *The point is this: the one who sows sparingly will also reap sparingly, and the one who sows bountifully will also reap bountifully.*

—2Corinthians 9:6

Our babies are created with souls of their own. As parents, we must remember to foster keeping the soul aspect of our children in balance with their other needs: physical, intellectual, and emotional.

One way, of course, means continuing as a family to attend weekly Mass regularly. Children grow accustomed to the holiness of the sanctuary. Undoubtedly, encouraging children towards comfort with and even affection for the sanctuary likely implies patience and determination in investing the child in quiet behavior. With prayer and perseverance, the adjustment soon enough manifests.

Because we need the presence of our Lord in the Eucharist, our paramount commitment to attend Mass every week fulfills absolute fortification. To receive the body/blood/soul/divinity of Jesus represents the summit of our worship. And in order to receive the Eucharist, the Holy Eucharist, we must remain faithful to keeping ourselves holy. We can achieve the goal of keeping ourselves holy and accountable to God only through faithful participation. Regularly worshiping together unifies Christ's Church. We are one body with many members.

Regularly worshiping together unifies Christ's Church.

Mass time with our Lord requires such a small block of time, and yet, it qualifies as the most beneficial obligation we can incorporate into family life. The message we hear from the pulpit, the hymns we sing, and especially receiving Jesus as Eucharist in a proper state of grace transform us. Somehow, we leave the church building with a lighter step and a song in our hearts . . .

Children can also become involved by becoming altar servers actively assisting the priest. Boys and girls generally from grade four through high school have the necessary maturity and willingness to learn all helpful tasks at the priest's side at the altar in preparation for the Eucharistic celebration. Serving in that way honors the child and fosters the deepening of a call to serve our Lord with all one's gifts of time, helpfulness, and care.

Through Jesus's life, death, and resurrection
comes our greatest light, our eternal hope.

public domain photo courtesy of Pexels.com

Defending Our Faith

To think that our times have become too difficult to navigate constitutes not an issue only in our current times. Faith has carried us through hundreds of generations, beginning with the Israelites, the Jews, God's chosen people. Scripture contains wisdom that recognizes false teachings and instruction about how to overcome evil with good.

Let us not forget how the coming of our Messiah, Jesus Christ, brought powerful light and hope into our world. Through Jesus's life, death, and resurrection comes our greatest light, our eternal hope—if only we believe and keep our hearts soft and supple in the love God has for us.

Imagine a day without light. Imagine living without hope: no kindness with no love of neighbor plus no hope, with no love for God and all he created.

What happens in our world when there is no hope? How do our children fare? Combine less hope with another ploy, distraction, and young people not only do not know how to handle hopelessness, but many resort to giving in to their demons in one of many forms of escapism. Here is the area that parents fear most, and rightly so. Parents are wise to face the reality. It helps to reflect upon the physical, mental, and spiritual consequences of such harm.

public domain photo courtesy of Pexels.com

Right now, society experiences lack of light and lack of love. Lacking those necessary fundamentals for living, we find ourselves with less strength or faith, less compassion or love, and less discipline or obedience. The waning of such disciplines inevitably leads only to one thing: less hope.

Do you recall the Genesis account of the fall of man? At the beginning of creation, the first unruly angel in the heavens, Lucifer, had thought himself to be as great as God. Named by God the angel of light because of his beauty, Lucifer became caught up in selfish pride and thereby was cast out of God's presence in heaven.

The knowledge of good and evil is no fairy tale or myth. Do we give enough thought to the effect such powerful pride has in our world? Lucifer, God's favored angel renamed as Satan for his pride and betrayal, has been loosed on the earth and prowls among us.

The crux of the matter concerns good and evil. Satan knows he is damned from Heaven. In his pride and jealousy, he wants others also to be damned from God's favor and the promise of Heaven, so he lures people away by all sorts of methods, sometimes subtle, sometimes not. Satan does not care whether or not you worship him, as long as you do not believe in worshiping the Almighty God, who punished Lucifer appropriately by banishing him to hell.

All Satan's nefarious methods lead to ruination of souls and destruction of all kinds, beginning with the Original Sin of Adam and Eve, causing physical death and eternal damnation for humans.

God loves all creatures, but the absolute righteousness of God also manifests justice, as God is perfect and holy.

Our loving God's sovereignty reigns above all, and we must accept that truth and await the Blessed Hope of the glory of eternal life in God's plan for our spiritual salvation.

> *Cast away from you all the transgressions that you have committed against me, and get yourselves a new heart and a new spirit! Why will you die, O house of Israel? For I have no pleasure in the death of anyone, says the Lord God. Turn, then, and live.*
>
> —Ezekiel 18:31-32

Once we grow in understanding that God loves us despite our failings and that he freely offers his mercy and grace to us, we can begin to unbraid the twistedness of Satan's subtle arrogance. The Prophet Isaiah speaks of it, saying,

> *Ah, you who call evil good and good evil,*
> *who put darkness for light and light for darkness,*
> *who put bitter for sweet and sweet for bitter!*
>
> —Isaiah 5:20

History has dubbed the fallen angel with many titles, including: Father of Lies, Prince of Lies, Prince of Darkness, The Great Deceiver . . . Serpent. Devils and demons follow Satan. Not physical beings, they nevertheless harbor the sole intention of turning God's creation upside down by casting doubt into human consciences.

As Christians—as children of God—we must guard against such cunning and deception. Progressively, beliefs such as atheism and agnosticism deceive. So do concepts such as relativism and pelagianism, the heresy holding that humans do not need God to distinguish between good and evil. Both relativism and pelagianism incorrectly take

Avoid Relativism's Deceptive Trap

Relativism, according to a sermon given by Cardinal Joseph Ratzinger before his election as Pope Benedict VI from 2005 to 2013, is letting oneself be tossed and swept along by every wind of teaching and often looks like the only attitude acceptable to today's standards. We are moving towards a dictatorship of relativism that does not recognize anything as certain and which has as its highest goal one's own ego and one's own desires. However, as parents of CCD students, we have a different goal: the Son of God, true man. He is the measure of true humanism. Being an adult means having a faith that does not follow the waves of today's fashions or the latest novelties. A faith deeply rooted in friendship with Christ is adult and mature. It is friendship with Christ that opens us up to all that is good and gives us the knowledge to judge true from false, and deceit from truth.

their truths from individualism or narcissism. And then we witness the growing political battle that prefers secularization, which we must recognize as the evil it is as revealed to us in Holy Scripture.

Satan's wicked strategies creep in subtly and take insidious root. With each passing generation, the wicked choke weeds germinate a burgeoning garden of desensitization, coming at us in all directions and causing physical and moral decay.

We may have an uneasy feeling in our work lives and social circles. More so, our school-aged children feel the pull of spiritual and moral apathy in their social environments and in their forms of entertainment. Therefore, we must use all available spiritual tools to uphold our faith and the faith and overall well-being of our children. The full armor of our Catholic religion equips us in today's darkening moments:

public domain photo courtesy of Shutterstock

Satan's wicked strategies creep in subtly and take insidious root.

*Stand, therefore, and fasten the belt of Truth around
your waist, and put on the breastplate of Righteousness.
As shoes for your feet put on whatever will make you ready
to proclaim the gospel of Peace. With all of these, take the
shield of Faith, with which you will be able to quench
all the flaming arrows of the evil one. Take the helmet of
Salvation, and the sword of the Spirit, which is the word
of God.*

—Ephesians 6:14-17

Carrying the torch from our own formation takes a
great deal of fortitude.

*Beloved, I do not consider that I have made it my own;
but this one thing I do: forgetting what lies behind and
straining forward to what lies ahead, I press on towards
the goal for the prize of the heavenly call of God in Christ
Jesus. Let those of us then who are mature be of the same
mind; and if you think differently about anything, this too
God will reveal to you. Only let us hold fast to what we
have attained."*

—Philippians 3:13-16

Let's think of the Olympic Games for a moment. Does not the torch bearer carrying the heavy object bring forth the wholeness of a burning flame? Such light and heat conveys the spirit of the games, attentively maintained and held high with eyes on the goal—the ceremonial basin that will endure throughout the games for all the peoples of the world. The bearer forsakes fatigue while looking only straight ahead and staying the course.

Carrying the faith, especially as parents, resembles a torchbearer's run. For those with faith as strong as an ox, entrusting in God means the burden feels light as we rely on God's love and grace. Everyone can get there, as well.

Jesus says in Matthew 11:28-30,

> *Come to me, all you that are weary and are carrying heavy burdens, and I will give you rest. Take my yoke upon you, and learn from me; for I am gentle and humble in heart, and you will find rest for your souls. For my yoke is easy, and my burden is light.*

When we take that thought to heart, we shall know strength like no other. Adults and children alike need only take those first couple of baby steps toward such trust.

Morals: Fruits of The Holy Spirit

The fruit of the Spirit is Love, Joy, Peace, Patience, Kindness, Goodness, Faithfulness, Gentleness, and Self-control. There is no law against such things. And those who belong to Christ Jesus have crucified the flesh with its passions and desires. If we live by the Spirit, let us also be guided by the Spirit. Let us not become conceited, competing against one another, envying one another.

—Galatians 5:22-26

How does one speak to parents about such a personal matter as the responsibility of teaching about morals to their own children? Yet, teaching children about morality may be a parent's most important obligation.

Inculcating good morals into the value system of one's children may feel daunting, to be sure. Rest assured, our Almighty Father and our Blessed Mother Mary fully know the moral bidding of parental diplomacy we face every single day as we seek to instill ethical and moral responsibility in the lives of our children.

Sometimes we fail either by what we say or don't say or by what we do or don't do. Perhaps we have given in to our own weaknesses and, thus, fail to serve our children sufficiently.

Let us not wilt in weakness. Let us not doubt God's abundant grace to bring us sufficiently up to the task. He assures us in 2Corinthians that his grace prevails sufficient for us, because his power perfectly reveals itself in weakness.

With trust in God's will and the power of the Holy Spirit, we may find ourselves victorious in raising our children to possess good moral consciences. In the Book of

Luke, Jesus speaks plainly and truthfully of the need for God's compass, to his disciples,

> *So I say to you, ask, and it will be given to you; search, and you will find it; knock, the door will be opened. Is there anyone among you who, if your child asks for a fish, will give a snake instead of a fish? Or if the child asks for an egg, will give a scorpion? If you then, who are evil, know how to give good gifts to your children, how much more will the heavenly Father give the Holy Spirit to those who ask him?*
>
> —Luke 11:9-13

Bringing children to CCD takes an excellent step toward developing their understanding of God and God's true love for his children.

Wonderful is the opportunity for children to absorb, freely and without fear of rejection, all that can be handed down to them in the centuries-old history of Christ and the redemption of his Church. At CCD, your children learn many inspirational aspects about the saints that came before them, who grew in virtue exponentially by their lives and often by their martyr deaths. Children come to know the sacredness of a spiritual realm and of the Sacraments so necessary for indemnification—that is, to make whole: their bodies, minds, and souls. Through all the classes of CCD, your child becomes formed and informed for readiness to receive the Sacraments of the Church. The rest, dear brothers and sisters in Christ, is up to parents who want what's best for them.

No human author, no teacher has the same ultimate responsibility as a child's parents. The realization that parents come to know is that children continuously learn.

Therefore, parents must ceaselessly foster the realm of teaching and learning in all areas of their children's lives. To reiterate, it is never too early and it is never too late, similarly, to nurture the spiritual relationship between the child and God, the eternal parent. However, the time is now . . .

Consider the institution that is our Roman Catholic Church as a great garden shed. It contains a treasure trove of the Master Gardener's wisdom for each of us in this life and the next. We have the tools, naturally and supernaturally, we may draw from to yield fruits of the Spirit which shall lead to the child's vitality of today and the blessedness of eternal salvation rather than everlasting darkness and the parchedness of doom.

If we've ever wondered why our little bundles of joy don't come with an instruction manual, we would be wrong to imagine they don't. The instruction manual exists, and it is called The Holy Bible. You have nothing to fear when applying the great truths that we learn either by reading the Good Book or by attentively participating in the liturgies and listening to the gospels during Mass.

In the freedom of knowing God's love for us and with confidence that He knows what is truly good for us, a set of good morals is better attained with an open mind and heart. Keeping in that vein, morals veritably are less about the "don'ts." Instead, they are more about the "do's" of a willing heart!

Success begins with unfaltering faith that radiates to our children and beams evident in relationships with everyone around us: our families, our neighbors, and even to strangers or someone in need with kindness shown to them.

In his address to the throngs at World Youth Day, our Pope Francis stated, "It is good to do no wrong, but it is wrong to do no good."

Look up to the nighttime sky, and what do you behold? Ever the expanse, ever the brilliant glimmers that suggest but a hint of the wonders and glory of God—just an infinitesimal cache of some of God's golden nuggets of wisdom.

public domain photo courtesy of Pexels.com

Ever the expanse, ever the brilliant glimmers that suggest but a hint of the wonders and glory of God.

Regarding *LOVE*

Love is patient; love is kind; love is not envious or boastful or arrogant or rude. It does not insist on its own way; it is not irritable or resentful. It does not rejoice in wrongdoing, but rejoices in the truth. It bears all things, believes all things, hopes all things, endures all things.
—1Corinthians 3:4-7

Hatred stirs up strife, but love covers all offenses.

—Proverbs 10:12

. . . Therefore, I tell you, her sins, which were many, have been forgiven; hence she has shown great love. But the one to whom little is forgiven, loves little.

—Luke 7:47

Regarding *PEACE*

If it is possible, so far as it depends on you, live peaceably with all.

—Romans 12:18

Since we are justified by faith, we have peace with God through our Lord Jesus Christ, through whom we have obtained access to such grace in which we stand; and we boast in our hope of sharing the glory of God. And not only that, but we also boast in our sufferings, knowing that suffering produces endurance, and endurance produces character, and character produces hope, and hope does not disappoint us, because God's love has been poured into our hearts through the Holy Spirit that has been given to us.

—Romans 5:1-5

A tranquil mind gives life to the flesh, but passion makes the bones rot.

—Proverbs 14:30

Regarding *PATIENCE*

Endure trials for the sake of discipline. God is treating you as children; for what child is there whom a parent does not discipline? Moreover, we have human parents to discipline us, and we respected them. Should we not be even more willing to be subject to the Father of spirits and live? For they disciplined us for a short time as seemed best to them, and he disciplines us for our good, in order that we may share his holiness. Now, discipline always

*seems painful rather than pleasant at the time, but later it
yields the peaceful fruit of righteousness to those who have
been trained by it.*

—Hebrews 12:7,9-11

*My brothers and sisters, whenever you face trials of
any kind, consider it nothing but joy, because you know
that the testing of your faith produces endurance; and let
endurance have its full effect, so that you may be mature
and complete, lacking in nothing.*

—James 1:2-3

*Better is the end of a thing than its beginning; the
patient in spirit are better than the proud in spirit.*

—Ecclesiastes 7:8

Regarding *KINDNESS*

*The good person out of the good treasure of the heart
produces good, and the evil person out of the evil treasure
produces evil; for it is out of the abundance of the heart
that the mouth speaks.*

—Luke 6:45

*Like good stewards of the manifold grace of God, serve
one another with whatever gift each of you has received.*

—1Peter 4:10

*In everything do to others as you would have them do
to you; for this is the law and the prophets.*

—Matthew 7:12

Regarding *GOODNESS*

*Who is wise and understanding among you? Show by
your good life that your works are done with gentleness,
born out of wisdom . . . but the wisdom from above is first
pure, then peaceable, gentle, willing to yield, full of mercy
and good fruits, without a trace of partiality or hypocrisy.*

—James 3:13,17

Let mutual love continue. Do not neglect to show hospitality to strangers, for by doing that, some have entertained angels without knowing it.

—Hebrews 13:1-2

The eye is the lamp of the body. So, if your eye is healthy, your whole body will be full of light; but if your eye is unhealthy, your whole body will be full of darkness. If then the light in you is darkness, how great is the darkness!

—Matthew 6:22-23

Regarding *FAITHFULNESS*

For one believes with the heart and so is justified, and one confesses with the mouth and so is saved. The scripture says, "No one who believes in him will be put to shame." For, "Everyone who calls on the name of the Lord shall be saved."

—Romans 10:10-11,13

. . . But ask in faith, never doubting, for the one who doubts is like a wave of the sea, driven and tossed by the wind; for the doubter, being double-minded and unstable in every way, must not expect to receive anything from the Lord.

—James 1:6-7

Create in me a clean heart, O God, and put a new and right spirit within me. Do not cast me away from your presence, and do not take your holy spirit from me. Restore to me the joy of your salvation and sustain in me a willing spirit.

—Psalm 51:10-12

Regarding *GENTLENESS*

. . . Always be ready to make your defence to anyone who demands from you an account of the hope that is in you; yet do it with gentleness and reverence. Keep your

conscience clear, so that, when you are maligned, those who abuse you for your good conduct in Christ may be put to shame.

—1Peter 3:15-16

A soft answer turns away wrath, but a harsh word stirs up anger.

—Proverbs 15:1

You must understand this, my beloved: let everyone be quick to listen, slow to speak, slow to anger; for your anger does not produce God's righteousness. Therefore rid yourselves of all sordidness and rank growth of wickedness, and welcome with meekness the implanted word that has the power to save your souls.

—James 1:19-21

Regarding *SELF-CONTROL*

Beloved, never avenge yourselves, but leave room for the wrath of God; for it is written, 'Vengeance is mine, I will repay, says the Lord . . . ' Do not be overcome by evil, but overcome evil with good.

—Romans 12:19,21

Take care! Be on your guard against all kinds of greed; for one's life does not consist in the abundance of possessions.

—Luke 12:15

Conduct yourselves wisely towards outsiders, making the most of the time. Let your speech always be gracious, seasoned with salt, so that you may know how you ought to answer everyone.

—Colossians 4:5-6

. . . reuniting with the Church for true Christian vitality . . .
. . . realizing the Fullness of Our Faith . . . awaken to re-awaken . . .
. . . realigning hearts and minds . . . remaining strong to defend our Faith . . .
. . . recognizing relativism in a culture of decay . . .
. . . guarding and regarding God's desire for our true happiness . . .
. . . renewing ourselves . . . . revitalizing relationships . . .

public domain photo courtesy of Shutterstock.com

What Is the Mass?

Until the ministry of Jesus, the Almighty Father's gift of mercy was offered only to the Jews, the twelve tribes of Israel. With the crucifixion and resurrection of Jesus, the Father extended his saving grace to all people through his Son's fulfillment of the Old Covenant. Salvation and redemption through Jesus Christ define the New Covenant.

We should appreciate and devote ourselves to all that Jesus Christ, our Emmanuel, meaning God with us, came to do in his earthly ministry. Jesus's faithful apostles would continue the mission of his Church after Christ's death and resurrection by spreading the good news to the ends of the earth—to Gentiles as well as Jews.

For a little bit of background, let's better understand sacrifice and sanctification in earlier times. Under Jewish laws, feast days were commanded and religiously observed. The only way to atone for the sins of Jews required offering up lambs and other animals as burnt offerings pleasing to God. God chose the Levite tribe of Israel as high priests to take the sacrificial offerings and prepare them in exacting specificity according to law.

Everything in Jesus's three years of ministry, up to and including the Last Supper, had special ceremonial purpose. Our Lord expected to offer himself up once and for all as a sacrifice like the lamb of the Old Covenant to atone for the sins of mankind. Henceforth, all people, Jew or Gentile, could acknowledge Jesus as the Son of God who came to redeem them and worship him in spirit and truth.

Jesus willingly became the sacrificial lamb, prime and without defect. No bones shall break, according to the prophecy, and yet, death will come. The blood of Jesus would be poured out for many in order, as the apostles said, to fulfill scripture.

As Jesus broke bread, he said to his apostles, "Take this, all of you, and eat of it, for this is my body, which is to be given up for you." Likewise, he lifted up the cup and said, "Take this, all of you, and drink from it, for this is the chalice of my blood, the blood of the new and eternal covenant, which will be poured out for you and for many for the forgiveness of sins. Do this in memory of me." In so doing, he transformed the blood sacrifice of the Old Covenant into the redemptive sacrifice of the New Covenant while also replicating the bread and wine sharing common to all Jewish services for hundreds of years.

When the Holy Spirit descended on the apostles in an awesomely powerful way at Pentecost, they gained the courage to preach the Gospel to far corners of the known world. They continued the communion ritual for the growing Church in mass celebrations. Our Catholic Church constitutes the apostolic succession. Partaking in the Bread of Life consecrated at every Mass gives assurance of our salvation.

The Mass fulfills the purpose of nourishing our faith with the Bread of Life in the practice of worshiping God together as a community, and Catholics honor the commandment to participate in Sunday Mass and Mass on Holy Days of Obligation. Also, we may choose to participate in daily Mass. We must never forget the love and invaluable mercy of what God in three persons gave us. God gave Jesus and the Spirit as divine promise. Our hope lasts forever, from our lives in human form on earth to abundant life for all eternity.

The Mass fulfills the purpose of nourishing our faith with the Bread of Life in the practice of worshiping God together as a community

Eucharist is holy. The consecrated host equals living sacrifice. Our hearts, minds, and souls must revere the body, blood, soul, and divinity of our Savior, Jesus Christ. Awesome and abundant is God's grace in the Paschal Mystery, the resurrection of Jesus on Easter Sunday three days after his crucifixion and death.

To participate in the sacred celebration at least weekly offers us the opportunity to retract ourselves from the routines of our lives as we join together to refresh our minds, renew our spirits, and realign our focus. Just as importantly, we gather together in worship of our triune God: Father, Son, and Holy Spirit. When we enter the church, the house of the Lord both in body and in spirit, we shall reemerge with genuine blessings of peace and rejuvenation to go about the busyness of our families and work lives throughout the week.

The Mass

The Mass is holy and beautiful, a timeless tradition instituted for our necessity and to the glory of our God. A font of holy water, previously blessed, provides the first act of participating, and we should take advantage of it. We dip our right-hand fingers in the water and bless ourselves with the sign of the cross to remember the commitment and blessing of our own baptisms.

Upon selecting our pew, each of us shows reverence by genuflecting, that is, bending the right knee toward the floor and blessing ourselves with the sign of the cross as we look forward toward the altar with Christ's crucifixion and the tabernacle holding the Eucharist. Before Mass begins, we kneel in silent personal prayer to focus our minds, prepare our hearts, and ready our spirits.

Overview of the Mass
Introductory Rites

Introductory rites of the Mass include a procession of the celebrant and others to the altar in song followed by a greeting by the priest. Everyone makes the sign of the cross, followed by a communal penitential rite and priest's prayer of absolution. The priest leads the congregation in singing or speaking the Gloria, an appropriate beginning of our participation by glorifying God in song from heart to lips.

Liturgy of the Word
Scripture Reading

Based on a three-year cycle, several readings from both the Old Testament and the New Testament provide spiritual food gathered comprehensively.

First Reading from the Old Testament except at Easter Time
Responsorial Psalm
Second Reading from the New Testament
Gospel Reading

Gospel reading by priest or deacon from the gospel books of Matthew, Mark, or Luke during Year A, B, or C plus the gospel book of John, which may be proclaimed in the Lenten season, Easter time, and other Feasts of the Lord. The congregation stands for the gospel reading, and we receive the message by simultaneously saying, "Glory to you, O Lord" while we bless ourselves with our right thumbs with small signs of the cross over our minds, over our lips, and over our hearts.

Homily

Either a priest or a deacon delivers the homily or sermon. The homily ties together the day's readings of Jesus's fulfillment of the law and prophets. But the Holy Spirit may prompt the priest or deacon to address a relevant pressing issue by means of a sermon.

Profession of Our Faith

Congregants read or recite together the Nicene Creed. If read or recited from the heart, proclaiming the creed in unison impacts us deeply.

Prayer of the Faithful

After professing our Faith, we then rely on the same Faith to present to God our needs, the needs of all peoples, and the needs of the whole world through Christ our Lord.

Essence of Holy Eucharist:
Real Presence of Christ, Body and Soul

On the eve of the summit of Jesus's ministry, the Last Supper became the first Mass as Jesus told his disciples,

I have eagerly desired to eat this Passover
with you before I suffer.
—Luke 22:15

Holding the bread in his own hands, Jesus then gave his body to his disciples. Jesus's imperative, "Do this in memory of me," imposes the sacred continuum of transformation, esteeming the Eucharist as a gift to us because Jesus wants to give us his Life in order to redeem humanity from eternal banishment from heaven.
Perpetually and sacramentally, Jesus keeps lowering or emptying himself to us. By transforming an act of violence into a sign of his self-giving love,
Jesus shows us he is not passive on the cross.
The Paschal Mystery, the mystical essence of the crucifixion followed by Jesus's resurrection from the dead on Easter Sunday, contains and demonstrates Jesus's love and obedience and enjoins us to his humility as what is seen while his divinity is hidden, in the Eucharist. By consecrating bread and wine, a priest transforms them into the very body and blood of Christ.
The consecration of the Eucharist anchors our liturgical life as Catholics, and the Eucharist embodies both the source and summit of our liturgy and lives of faith.

Liturgy of the Eucharist
Offertory

During the Presentation and Preparation of Gifts, congregants give a portion from their earnings as offerings in thanksgiving and to uphold the corporal mission of the Church. Designated congregants bring bread and wine for consecration.

Eucharistic Prayer

The Preface

After the Preface Prayer, offered by a priest on our behalf, we respond by saying or singing "Holy, Holy, Holy, Hosanna in the Highest . . . "

Consecration

Next, the congregation kneels as the priest says the Eucharistic Prayer during consecration of the bread and wine. Kneeling shows reverence and humility for the ordained mystery of the blessing of the gifts.

The Communion Rite

Lord's Prayer

The priest offers other prayers after consecration of the bread and wine. Then, as Jesus instructed his followers about how to pray, the congregation stands to recite the Lord's Prayer together. We may opt to do so with clasped hands of our family members lifted up to the Lord, as the act enhances the meaning of the Lord's Prayer. We understand that the unison recitation of Our Father—the Lord's Prayer—pleases our Lord.

Sign of Peace

During the Sign of Peace, we greet those around us, typically by shaking hands, as a show of unity and a sign of the Lord's peace within ourselves willingly extended to our brothers and sisters in Christ. And this sign of peace concludes in the "Lamb of God" invocation.

Lamb of God

Sung during the fraction rite when the priest breaks the bread during consecration, the Lamb of God prayer ends with the congregation kneeling until the priest calls us to the front of the altar for the reception of the Sacrament of Eucharist, often called Communion because the recipients get into communion with Christ as they receive him in the Eucharist. Thus those congregants in or remaining in a state of grace, and therefore without mortal sin because of proper confession, may partake of Holy Communion. After receiving the host, another name for bread transformed into the body of Christ and drinking wine transformed into the blood of Christ, we return to pews to kneel in silent prayer or listen to the hymn. After that reflection, the priest offers a Prayer after Communion.

Concluding Rites

Concluding Rites may begin with the Prayer to Saint Michael, the Archangel, followed by Final Greeting, Final Blessing, and Dismissal. As we go in peace, we sing an exit hymn followed by a personal reception for all, by our priest (and deacon) near the exit.

The Seven Sacraments and Their Classification

Baptism

Sacrament of Initiation

Baptism is the first Sacrament. In Baptism, because one is usually too young, someone other than oneself comes forward in the Church to present you before God unless one is an adult being baptized. So, since the recipients are usually babies, parents and godparents play an all-important role in the Sacrament of Baptism.

In Baptism, the one baptized receives new life in Christ. The practice of baptism by water commenced with John the Baptist immersing sinners who believed. He also baptized Jesus himself, who thereafter started his ministry. After Pentecost, Jesus's disciples carried out his command to go forth baptizing repentant believers in the name of the Father, and of the Son, and of the Holy Spirit.

The pouring of water in baptism takes away the original sin from the baptized person through the gift of sanctifying grace and new birth in the Holy Spirit.

God gives the precious gift of the life of the infant child to parents. And we know that, as a priority in the fragility of life, we must have our child anointed and blessed for sanctification in the journey of life on earth.

Penance
Sacrament of Healing and Initiation

Early in the elementary years, a child has personally acquired knowledge between good and bad deeds and between right and wrong behavior. For example, a child begins to see that hurting another by one's own actions may fracture one's relationship between oneself and one's neighbors, and especially with God. In the CCD program, the Grade 2 class prepares for the Sacrament of Penance.

With a repentant heart, one receives God's forgiveness through the Sacrament of Penance. God's healing grace comes through absolution by a priest, for Jesus tells his apostles,

If you forgive the sins of any, they are forgiven them; if you retain the sins of any, they are retained.

—John 20:23

Absolution by the priest completely cleans away one's sins in that the penitent no longer faces condemnation to hell as a consequence of sin, provided one sins no more thereafter.

The admission/confession of sin results in the priest's assessment of an appropriate penance, usually in the form of prayers and contemplation, to atone for our sins. After confession, which is necessary for our restoration back into the state of grace, we experience inner joy that culminates in our receiving Holy Eucharist with guilt-free hearts.

Eucharist • Holy Communion
Sacrament of Initiation

In a way, the Sacrament of Eucharist or Holy
Communion encapsulates the birth, ministry, persecution,
suffering, death, and resurrection of our Lord Jesus
Christ. In it, we relive the Paschal Mystery of Christ. In
the Eucharist, we receive Jesus Christ himself, the Living
Bread that came down from heaven to redeem humans
from sin. As we come to the table of the Lord for the
Eucharist, we partake of the Eucharist with a pure heart
and reverence, thus nourishing a life of faith that draws
us into the life of Christ himself.

Generally, a child reaches spiritual readiness for
the Sacrament of Eucharist at the age of seven. A child
receives First Communion after receiving First Penance.
Ordinarily, a child receives First Communion in Grade 2
with a group of other children and during a celebration
taking place in the context of the entire community of
faith, i.e., the Church.

Confirmation
Sacrament of Initiation

In the many years of spiritual growth and intellectual
maturity that follow First Communion, a junior in high
school may have reached viable age to be confirmed in
the faith. The intervening ten or so years prove crucial
for formation, both at home and at CCD classes, for the
young person who is likely encouraged to attend weekly
Mass and frequently receive the Sacraments of Penance
and Eucharist during these years of spiritual development
leading to the Sacrament of Confirmation.

The culmination of religious education at church and, indeed, of spiritual nurturing from parents at home is the strong foundation that is essential for a child's intellectual and spiritual well-being. Firm in a desire for wholeness and well-being, parents more fully realize the dimensions of their child in body, mind, and spirit. Now a young person has developed to the point of readiness for a special outpouring of the Holy Spirit through the Sacrament of Confirmation so that he or she can boldly and courageously face the challenges of life both spiritually and secularly in the world at-large.

> *Anointing and sealing in the*
> *Sacrament of Confirmation*
> *do not mark the end of a*
> *Catholic's sojourn with Catholic faith and practice.*
> *The Sacrament of Confirmation*
> *marks only a beginning.*

Praying and encouraging must continue, because age does not limit the life-affirming workings of God the Father, Son, and Holy Spirit in our children's journey into and during the adult years.

Holy Matrimony
Sacrament of Service

In the Sacrament of Holy Matrimony, a man and woman join together in love and completely give themselves to each other just as Jesus gives himself to his bride, the Church. A couple unified through Holy Matrimony embodies a deep and sacred relationship borne of love and trust that leads to salvation of souls.

Through the Sacrament of Holy Matrimony, a man and woman exchange vows and rings, and the two become one flesh, completing one another in body, mind, and spirit. By nature, the holy union is ordered toward the good of the spouses and the procreation and educating of children, who enrich the sanctified union of love, if God so blesses the couple with the gift of a child or children.

In light of their responsibilities within the community of faith and general society, a couple receives Holy Matrimony to serve each other, their children, the Church, and all humanity. Engaged couples will find it important to contact a priest well in advance to prepare for the Sacrament of Matrimony in order to gain a deeper understanding of the love and commitment of a healthy marriage through the eyes of the Church.

Couples must take marriage seriously and enter the vocation—a life calling—in genuine and mature love for each other.

Holy Orders
Sacrament of Service

Discernment of the vocation to Holy Orders demonstrates a call to serve God as a priest or deacon in the Church. Discernment in service of such a special nature moves men to offer themselves totally to God and the Church as ordained priests and deacons in a diocesan, religious, or monastic setting.

This kind of call to serve God and the Church goes back to the origins of Christ's Church as he picked the apostles from his disciples (Mark 3:13-19).

Serving the Lord through Holy Orders vitally supports the continuity of the Church.

Anointing of the Sick
Sacrament of Healing

In a special way, the Sacrament of Anointing of the Sick unites the pain and suffering of a sick person who receives it to the pain and suffering of Jesus during the events surrounding his crucifixion and death. A priest's laying on of hands and anointing with oil confers forgiveness, healing, and strength upon a person. The Sacrament of Anointing of the Sick ultimately acts for the salvation of the recipient, as it carries with it the forgiveness of sins. A loved one may request Anointing of the Sick for the gravely incapacitated Catholic. But it is preferable to call a priest before one's illness worsens because it is a Sacrament of the sick, not of the dying. Anointing is conferred for the healing of one's soul and the body—if God so wills.

Vitality of Formation
a personal message from Kathleen Bennett

Sometimes when I go to Mass, I look around at others as they ready themselves or participate. They come one or they come all, but they come.

Like my parents and grandparents before me, I experience Mass in all its holy facets just as they and presumably many generations before them did, even on different continents. In fact, they came to America in great part to worship freely. So tradition and common unity of the Catholic Church naturally connect me with anyone and everyone when I worship in the sanctuary of Christ's Church.

I'd like to share a little observation. In a different way than the world sees them, I notice things that adorn people—but not adornments the world typically sees. I can see a young mother's cloak of gentleness and her headdress of humility. Along with a placid smile, she wears a ring of love, a chain of passion, bangles of patience and persever-ance, and an attractive pair of contemplative earrings.

Elderly couples arrive together, their silver hair crowns of wisdom and their slow movements, loving and well-seasoned.

And then I think of my own life in so many years in between, going my own way—the years I strayed from God.

Train children in the right way, and when old, they will not stray.

—Proverbs 22:6

A simple proverb but so true.

My life's own progression can attest to that verse, Proverbs 22:6. Such a tiny passage and yet the passage of my thirty-plus years of having fallen away equal but the comma in Verse 6 of the Book of Proverbs, Chapter 22. I recall that era of being away from my beloved Catholic Church and living in the void. Many times, for years on end, I languished in the void.

Why did I go down the broad and easy roads that lead to destruction, and how did I eventually climb out of that vacuous hole?

> *Enter through the narrow gate, for the gate is wide and the road is easy that leads to destruction, and there are many who take it. For the gate is narrow and the road is hard that leads to life, and there are few who find it.*
> —Matthew 7:13-14

The past few decades seem notable and sad to me in a new light of seeing a decline of good Christian morals and values overall both in the secular world and even in the Catholic demographic. I cannot hold back my testimony, and I petition with prayer, asking, "Lord, how may I use my talent and passion for your glory? Who is my audience, and what is my message? Show me."

So my passion in creating a handbook for you, parents within the Church, propels my desire to help build up your faith and that of your families in our difficult world. What parents do not want what is good for their children? Of course, parents wish to spare their children from anguish and mere existence that languishes. Our Father and Mother in Heaven want no less for us, no matter our age, whether we are youngsters or parents ourselves.

The more I practice my faith, the more Psalm 51:10-12 echoes my soul.

> Create in me a clean heart, O God, and put a new
> and right spirit within me. Do not cast me away from
> your presence, and do not take your holy spirit from me.
> Restore to me the joy of your salvation, and sustain in me
> a willing heart.

—Psalm 51:10-12

I speak heart to heart, because that is all I have to offer. I possess neither a college nor theology degree. Simply, my spirit wells and appreciates the love and faithfulness of my God, the merciful redemption by his Son, Jesus Christ, and the most powerful and amazing strength, guidance, and peace of the Holy Spirit. I cannot hold back my testimony, for my joy reigns glorious yet inadequately expressible.

Perhaps people like me, who know well how such apathy degrades themselves individually and societally, once chose the easy road but eventually found it unbearable with emptiness and strife.

I discovered that one falls away by apathy and keeps away in atrophy.

Since coming back into the fold like a lowly lost sheep, I feel my Lord embracing me as I embrace my Catholic faith. I don't come to Mass because I am a saint. I come because I am a sinner. However, I love to be in communion with all the saints and martyrs before me, who exult with me from heaven, where my hope shines and my wholeness awaits.

The more I feed upon the Word of God, the more abundant my life. The more years I serve on the religious education board, the more I care about and pray for the spiritual strength, discipline, and courage of parents in our parish as they go about forming their children in faith. The entire board keeps families in their prayers.

Consider the Christian's call and election:

> *His divine power has given us everything needed for life and godliness, through the knowledge of him who called us by his own glory and goodness. Thus he has given us, through these things, his precious and very great promises, so that through them you may escape from the corruption that is in the world because of lust, and may become participants in the divine nature. For this very reason, you must make every effort to support your faith with goodness, and goodness with knowledge, and knowledge with self-control, and self-control with endurance, and endurance with godliness, and godliness with mutual affection, and mutual affection with love.*
> —2Peter, 1:3-7

Dear Sisters and Brothers, may we remember to draw on the anchors of our faith: the Church and her magisterial leadership from pope to priest, traditions, sacred scripture, and certainly not least, the Blessed Sacraments that sustain our relationships with almighty God and with humanity.

I urge you not to take for granted, even for a moment, all that can and should be shared with your family. Personally, I cannot fathom the lives of so many people in the world who give no consideration of bringing their children to God or imparting any such knowledge about the Creator of all. Hope is found only in the Light of God's goodness and eternal love.

You are on the path of Holy Sacraments with your children. May this book help you stay the course, exercise your faith, nourish your souls, and harden not your hearts lest the children languish outside of God's grace and abundant inheritance.

We've been given the Sacraments and myriad other tools for cultivating the culture of life and life eternal. Our pastor is just a phone call away to assist you or answer your questions. Finally, may this book aid you as you journey onward and journey upward.

Peace be with you always.

public domain photo courtesy of Shutterstock.com

You are on a path of holy sacraments with your children.

Common Prayers

Lord's Prayer

Our Father, who art in heaven, hallowed be thy name. Thy kingdom come. Thy will be done on earth as it is in heaven. Give us this day our daily bread and forgive us our trespasses, as we forgive those who trespass against us, and lead us not into temptation, but deliver us from evil. Amen.

Hail, Mary

Hail, Mary, full of grace, the Lord is with thee. Blessed art thou among women, and blessed is the fruit of thy womb, Jesus. Holy Mary, Mother of God, pray for us sinners, now and at the hour of our death. Amen.

Glory Be

Glory be to the Father and to the Son and to the Holy Spirit. As it was in the beginning, is now, and ever shall be, world without end. Amen.

Grace

a prayer before meals

Bless us, O Lord, and these thy gifts, which we are about to receive from thy bounty, through Christ, Our Lord. Amen.

Nicene Creed

I believe in one God, the Father almighty,
maker of heaven and earth,
of all things visible and invisible.
I believe in one Lord, Jesus Christ,
the Only Begotten Son of God,

(Nicene Creed continued on next page)

born of the Father before all ages.

God from God, Light from Light,

true God from true God,

begotten, not made, consubstantial with the Father;

through him, all things were made.

For us men and for our salvation

he came down from heaven,

and by the Holy Spirit was incarnate of the Virgin
    Mary,

and became man.

For our sake he was crucified under Pontius Pilate,

he suffered death and was buried,

and rose again on the third day

in accordance with the Scriptures.

He ascended into heaven and is seated

at the right hand of the Father.

He will come again in glory

to judge the living and the dead

and his kingdom will have no end.

I believe in the Holy Spirit, the Lord, the giver of life,

who proceeds from the Father and the Son,

who with the Father and the Son is adored and
    glorified,

who has spoken through the prophets.

I believe in one holy, catholic, and apostolic Church.

I confess one Baptism for the forgiveness of sins

and I look forward to the resurrection of the dead

and the life of the world to come. Amen.

Act of Contrition

My God, I am sorry for my sins with all my heart. In choosing to do wrong and failing to do good, I have sinned against you whom I should love above all things.

I firmly intend, with your help, to do penance, to sin no more, and to avoid whatever leads me to sin. Our Savior Jesus Christ suffered and died for us. In his name, my God, have mercy.

Prayer to Saint Michael

Saint Michael, the Archangel, defend us in battle, be our defense against the wickedness and snares of the devil. May God rebuke him, we humbly pray; and do thou, O Prince of the heavenly host, by the power of God, thrust into Hell Satan and the other evil spirits who prowl about the world for the ruin of souls. Amen.

When prayed in quietude and without distraction,
the Rosary evokes mystical power.

public domain photo courtesy of Shutterstock.com

History of the Rosary

The concept of the rosary stems from the inspiration experienced in the thirteenth century by Saint Dominic, reportedly from the Blessed Mother, Mary, herself.

The components that make up the Rosary's structure constitute a complete, simple, and deep flow of three forms of prayer: vocal, meditative, and contemplative. The Rosary presumably also provided the beads themselves as a useful tool for illiterate people in a time prior to individual education for the general public.

Today, the Holy Rosary of the Blessed Virgin Mary remains a staple in our worship. Truly, when prayed in quietude and without distraction, the Rosary evokes mystical power. With the aid of a set of rosary beads, repetition of each decade of prayers including one Lord's Prayer, ten Hail Marys, one Glory Be, and one Fatima Prayer reinforces familiarity through rhythm. From Saint Dominic's day to the year 1569 when the Church officially approved the Rosary prayer form, the Rosary developed.

With its complete summary of the life and ministry of Jesus, the Holy Rosary today serves as a loving invitation to Mary for her intercession with her son for each of us. Just as she taught her son to pray, she wishes us to pray and pray well as we meditate upon the face and sacred heart of Jesus, her son.

While praying the mysteries of the revelation, life, ministry, death, and resurrection of Jesus Christ—twenty in all— may overwhelm a person in one sitting, the Rosary is best prayed with only one of the four sets of mysteries contemplated at a time. The Mysteries are grouped in four sets as Joyful, Luminous, Sorrowful, and Glorious.

Mysteries of the Holy Rosary
Joyful Mysteries

First Joyful Mystery
The Annunciation

How unprecedented, for a young virgin pledged in marriage, to have a visit from the Angel Gabriel! How mystifying for Mary to consider that awesome responsibility and the potential modification of plans for her life! How faithful and obedient for Mary nonetheless to answer, "I am the handmaiden of the Lord. May your will be done to me!" To contemplate The Annunciation is to understand the bearing of fruit in the virtue of humility.

Second Joyful Mystery
The Visitation

After consenting to become the mother of God, Mary visited her much older cousin, Elizabeth, once thought barren but now in her sixth month of pregnancy. Elizabeth's baby, John the Baptist, leapt for joy in her womb as Jesus arrived in Mary's womb when Mary visited and greeted Elizabeth. By God's mysterious grace, Elizabeth knew that the baby in Mary's womb was the Lord and greeted Mary saying, "Blessed are you among women, and blessed is the fruit of your womb!"

To contemplate The Visitation leads to appreciating the love of neighbor that reaffirms and blesses both giver and receiver in acts of kindness.

Third Joyful Mystery
The Birth of Christ

As they travel to Bethlehem to register for a mandated census in her ninth month of pregnancy, Joseph and Mary know they carry the precious New Covenant entrusted to them in the form of Jesus in Mary's womb. Far away from home, she goes into labor, but no one has room for them anywhere in the village.

Someone suggested they find an enclosure in pastureland on the outskirts of the village. There, Mary gave birth, wrapped Jesus in swaddling clothes, and laid him in a makeshift crib: a straw-lined manger, a trough that could hold water for animals to drink.

To contemplate The Birth of Jesus begins the understanding

that our Messiah has come without fanfare into the world, taking on human flesh in a willing act of obedience and humility. Although the Messiah has been disregarded, discredited by his humble beginning, rejected by many, he also has been acknowledged and believed in by all who are faithful and encounter him in everyday living. Virtues found in the mystery of the Birth of Jesus include humility—and faith—as well as the evangelical counsel of poverty.

Even deeper, we may ponder the roles of ourselves as sheep and of Jesus as the Good Shepherd, who feeds us.

Fourth Joyful Mystery
The Presentation in the Temple

Jewish law commanded parents to consecrate their first-born male at the temple. How dutiful for Mary and Joseph to do so! They knew they had responsibility for the Son of God, An elder, out of all men at the temple in Jerusalem, took one look at the infant Jesus and recognized instantly the baby as the Christ Child.

To contemplate The Presentation is to see the virtue of obedience as a fruitful manifestation of always living by God's Word and trusting in the blessings of following the precepts of God.

Fifth Joyful Mystery
Finding the Child Jesus in the Temple

Imagine having lost a young son in the vast crowds amid bustling activity in the city, Jerusalem, far away from your country home in Nazareth! What a relief for his parents to find him! Jesus amazed even them that he would be exactly where he knew he should be— among people in the house of his Father.

To contemplate the Finding of Jesus in the Temple reflects exactly where we should be in the trials and discouragements that face us in our day-to-day lives. Once we find and cling to Jesus's Way, Truth, and Life, we have the consolable joy of finding him.

Luminous Mysteries

First Luminous Mystery

Baptism of Jesus

In the River Jordan, Jesus publicly showed us who he is, beginning with the waters of his Baptism. The Spirit of God, in the form of a dove, descended upon him. A voice from the heavens affirmed the sacred act for all to hear with the Father's words, "This is my beloved Son in whom I am well pleased." (Matthew 3:17)

To contemplate the Baptism of Jesus is to welcome the Holy Spirit in the life of the child born to you: the child's soul is a precious gift, as is the amazing grace bestowed at the time of the Sacrament of Baptism.

Second Luminous Mystery

Jesus Changes Water into Wine at the Wedding at Cana

At Mother Mary's prompting, Jesus performed his first miracle. Because wine ran out during the wedding feast, he summoned men to fill nearby jugs of water. Jesus turned the water into an abundance of choicest wine, and many noted that the host had saved the best for last.

To contemplate the miracle at the Wedding at Cana offers opportunities for meditation. First, we may ask for Mary's intercession with her son, Jesus, for our needs and the needs of others. Then, we may offer up what few temporal things we already have, with faith in God's generosity, which abounds in ways profoundly deeper than we can imagine.

Third Luminous Mystery

Proclaiming of the Kingdom

Jesus's followers witnessed Jesus's Way, Truth, and Life, and were forever changed by the emerging New Covenant. Jesus's call to us to repent because the Kingdom of God is at hand was a clear manifestation that the salvation of our lives lies in believing in him and his Message. It is only then that we are assured of entrance into the heavenly kingdom.

To contemplate the Proclamation of the Kingdom is to trust in the ways and workings of the Holy Trinity. We must acknowledge that we fall short of God's glory and must repent for the sins that separate us from Him. We share that truth and pray for those we care about who do not know the way yet or may just be blind to it.

Fourth
Luminous Mystery
The Transfiguration

What a mysterious, unparalleled sight for Jesus's closest disciples to see the Transfiguration of Jesus with Elijah and Moses atop the mountain! Jesus's countenance shone extraordinarily brilliant. That dazzling yet brief glimpse of God's glory forged an indelible witness for the apostles Peter,

James, and John.

To contemplate The Transfiguration means holding onto our desire for holiness and to the promise of the glories of eternal life in heaven.

Fifth
Luminous Mystery
Institution of the Eucharist

Jesus instructed his disciples at the Last Supper to break bread in communion and drink from the cup of wine. He told them that the bread and wine transformed into his body and blood are given and poured out for them and for many, for the New Covenant.

To contemplate the Eucharist, as pre-ordained by the sacrificial Lamb, reminds us that the covenantal atoning character of the Eucharist remains a supernatural mystery of the living bread. Our eternal Savior deserves reverence and adoration.

Sorrowful Mysteries

First Sorrowful Mystery

Agony in the Garden

Our sins and the need to take away the sins of the world dwelt heavily in Jesus's heart. During his abandonment by his sleeping disciples after the Last Supper, Jesus prayed intensely and sweated blood, knowing all that he would soon suffer.

Contemplating the Agony in the Garden enables us to acknowledge that our own sinfulness brings Jesus sorrow and suffering. It also makes us realize the debt of eternal gratitude we ought to feel for God's plan of salvation for us.

Second Sorrowful Mystery

Scourging at the Pillar

The Roman procurator Pontius Pilate ordered Jesus beaten with whips and metal balls affixed to chains.

In contemplating the Scourging, we know that our Lord has taken the beating for our wrongdoing. Even though his purity has purified us, we must fathom the sense of hurt we cause him when we give in to our sins.

Third Sorrowful Mystery

Crowning with Thorns

When the tormentors crown him with thorns, our Redeemer endures still more external and internal pain.

To contemplate the Crowning with Thorns means seeing Jesus's abundant humility and that, with his humility, we are beholden to his courage.

Fourth Sorrowful Mystery

Carrying the Cross

His persecutors told the already physically weakened Jesus that he must carry the cross on which he'd be crucified up to the site of his crucifixion, Golgotha or the Place of the Skull. Carrying the cross comprised Jesus's own mode of atonement.

When Jesus fell, the persecutors ordered Simon of Cyrene, a man in the crowd, to bear the burden, taking up the cross for a short duration so that Jesus could regain enough physical strength to endure to the end despite two more falls.

To contemplate the Carrying of the Cross reminds us of the pain in Jesus's suffering. At the same time, the faithful, too, realize that they bear a cross when they suffer. Through suffering, we grow in the virtues of patience and endurance.

Fifth Sorrowful Mystery

Crucifixion and Death

Father, into your hands I commend my spirit," said Jesus in his last human breath.

—Luke 23:46

To contemplate the Crucifixion encourages valuing and striving for perseverance like the perseverance of Jesus. Let us remember that heaven awaits the faithful who endure to the end.

Glorious Mysteries

First Glorious Mystery
Resurrection

After death and burial, our Lord rose in a supernatural way. Jesus Christ visited his followers in several glorious appearances.

In contemplation of the Resurrection, who can fathom the power to rise up? How breathtaking and reaffirming to have seen the resurrected Jesus! We, too, believe that the ascendant victory fulfills our Savior's mission of redeeming us from the power of sins as it reaffirms our faith.

Second Glorious Mystery
Ascension to Heaven

The Father takes our Savior up into the clouds and back to heaven after he spends forty days on the earth in his mystical form witnessed by many, after his Resurrection.

To contemplate the Ascension to Heaven, imagine the inexplicable magnificence of the moment. Realizing that Jesus has made our own entry into God's presence in heaven possible, may we rest in hope for our own afterlives in the gloriousness of heaven.

Third Glorious Mystery
Descent of the Holy Spirit

As our Savior returns to heaven, he fulfills a promise to his apostles: he fills them with the Holy Spirit so that they become on fire to proclaim the Gospel to all peoples in their native tongues.

As we contemplate the Descent of the Holy Spirit, we realize that we share in the gift through our baptism and our confirmation in the Spirit at the threshold of our coming of age. The Holy Spirit blesses us when we call upon him for guidance, enlightenment, strength, and consolation—the powerful gift of God's love.

Fourth Glorious Mystery
Assumption of Mary

Mother of God, Arc of the Covenant. Mary's faithfulness and willingness to live by the Word of God renders her a saint like no other. How fitting that God assumes her body into heaven without the decay of physical death!

To contemplate the Assumption of Mary brings us to another mystery of God's glory and good pleasure, the grace of a happy death.

Fifth Glorious Mystery
Coronation of Mary

As revealed in the Book of Revelation, a great sign appeared in the sky: a woman clothed with the sun, the moon under her feet, and on her head, a crown of twelve stars. It could be no other than our Queen Mother, Mary, given to us in a special way at the foot of the cross by Jesus himself.

To contemplate the Coronation of Mary leads us to recognize the special favor God bestowed upon her among all people and to trust in Mary's intercession as we petition for prayers for ourselves and others. All who entrust themselves as her children eventually realize that our spiritual mother so desires us to persevere so that we may know the unsearchable riches of our Lord and Savior.

How to Pray the Rosary

For whom, or what, specifically would you like to pray? Keep that intention for Mary's intercession on your heart, and use the beads to guide your prayer, as follows:

Hold the Crucifix on the beads between your thumb and two or three other fingers.

Make the Sign of the Cross. The right hand touches the forehead when you say the words "In the name of the Father . . . ," the hand touches the chest for the words ". . . and of the Son . . . ," the hand touches the left shoulder for the words ". . . and of the Holy . . . ," and the hand touches the right shoulder on the word ". . .Spirit." Incidentally, your grandmother or grandfather may have learned to say ". . . and of the Holy Ghost." Then, clasp hands in prayer for the word, "Amen," which means, "So be it."

Say the Apostles Creed on the Crucifix.

On the bead closest to the Crucifix, say the Our Father.

On each of the next three, smaller beads, offer one Hail Mary on each bead.

On the chain before the next large bead, say the Glory Be prayer.

While still holding the chain, before each mystery say the Fatima Prayer, O, My Jesus.

Announce the First Mystery of the set you choose on the next large bead. Then say the Our Father.

Say a Hail Mary on each of the next ten beads.

Say the Glory Be prayer on the chain after the ten Hail Marys.

Then say the Fatima Prayer, O, My Jesus.

On the next large bead, announce the next Mystery of the set you've chosen.

Continue with that sequence through each series of ten beads, each series called decade, and announce a new Mystery in turn from the chosen set. When you return to the medal, say the prayer Hail, Holy Queen.

At the conclusion of Hail, Holy Queen, return to the Crucifix, and say the optional closing prayer.

Then, make the Sign of the Cross.

Texts of Rosary Prayers

Sign of the Cross

In the name of the Father and of the Son and of the
Holy Spirit. Amen.

Apostles Creed

I believe in God, the Father almighty, Creator of
heaven and earth, and in Jesus Christ, his only Son, our
Lord, who was conceived by the Holy Spirit, born of the
Virgin Mary, suffered under Pontius Pilate, was crucified,
died, and was buried. He descended into hell. On the
third day, he rose again from the dead. He ascended into
heaven and is seated at the right hand of God, the Father,
almighty. From there, he will come to judge the living and
the dead.

I believe in the Holy Spirit, the holy catholic Church,
the communion of saints, the forgiveness of sins, the
resurrection of the body, and life everlasting. Amen.

The Lord's Prayer or Our Father

Our Father, who art in heaven, hallowed be thy name.
Thy kingdom come. Thy will be done on earth as it is in
heaven. Give us this day our daily bread, and forgive us
our trespasses as we forgive those who trespass against
us; and lead us not into temptation, but deliver us from
evil. Amen.

Hail, Mary

Hail, Mary, full of grace, the Lord is with thee. Blessed
art thou among women, and blessed is the fruit of thy

womb, Jesus. Holy Mary, Mother of God, pray for us sinners, now and at the hour of our death. Amen.

Glory Be

Glory be to the Father, and to the Son, and to the Holy Spirit. As it was in the beginning, is now, and ever shall be, world without end. Amen.

O, My Jesus, the Fatima Prayer

O, my Jesus, forgive us our sins. Save us from the fires of hell. Lead all souls to heaven, especially those in most need of thy mercy.

Hail, Holy Queen

Hail, Holy Queen, Mother of Mercy, our life, our sweetness, and our hope. To thee do we cry, poor banished children of Eve. To thee do we send up our sighs, mourning and weeping in this vale of tears. Turn, then, most Gracious Advocate, thine eyes of mercy toward us, and after this our exile, show unto us the blessed fruit of thy womb, Jesus.

O clement, O loving, O sweet Virgin Mary, pray for us, O holy Mother of God, that we may be made worthy of the promises of Christ.

O, God
A Closing Prayer

O, God, whose only-begotten Son by his life, death, and resurrection has purchased for us the rewards of eternal life, grant, we beseech thee, that while meditating on these sacred mysteries of the most holy Rosary of the Blessed Virgin Mary, we may imitate what they contain and obtain what they promise. Through the same Christ our Lord. Amen.

The Ten Commandments

1. I am the LORD, your God: you shall not have strange gods before me. You shall not make to thyself any graven thing; nor the likeness of anything that is in heaven above, nor in the earth beneath, nor of those things that are in the waters under the earth. You shall not adore them nor serve them.

2. You shall not take the name of the LORD, your God, in vain.

3. Remember to keep holy the LORD's Day.

4. Honor your father and mother.

5. You shall not kill.

6. You shall not commit adultery.

7. You shall not steal.

8. You shall not bear false witness against your neighbor.

9. You shall not covet your neighbor's wife.

10. You shall not covet your neighbor's goods.

The Parables
Teachable Moments with your Children

In the Gospels of Matthew, Mark, and Luke, Jesus demonstrates teachings to the disciples or larger crowds in the form of parables. In answer to many questions, Jesus used parables as a way to illustrate a situation by using everyday people, places, or things. The impactful teachings by our Lord resonate just as well today as they did in the first century.

You will find parables in your Holy Bible:

public domain photo
courtesy of Pexels.com

The Parable of the . . .
Fig Tree, Luke 13:6-9
Good Samaritan, Luke 10:25-37
Great Banquet, Luke 14:15-24
Growing Seed, Mark 4:26-29
Hidden Treasure, The Pearl,
    Matthew 13:44-46
Lost Coin, Luke 15:8-10
Lost Sheep,
    Matthew 18:10-14, • Luke 15:1-7
Mustard Seed and Yeast,
Matthew 13:31-43, • Mark 4:30-33
    Luke 13:18-19
Net, Matthew 13:47-52
Persistent Widow, Luke 18:1-8
Pharisee & Tax Collector
    Luke 18:9-14
Prodigal Son., Matthew 21:28-32

(parables continued on next page)

(parables continued from previous page)

Rich Fool, Luke 12:13-21

Shrewd Manager, Luke 16:1-15

Sower, Matthew 13:1-23

   Mark 4:1-25 • Luke 8:1-15

Talents, Matthew 25:14-30

Ten Gold Coins, Luke 19:11-27

Ten Virgins, Matthew 25:1-33

Tenants, Matthew 21:33-46

   Mark 12:1-17, • Luke 20:9-19

Unmerciful Servant

   Matthew 18:21-35

Wedding Banquet, Matthew 22:1-14

Weeds, Matthew 13:24-30

Workers in the Vineyard

   Matthew 20:1-16

Yeast, Luke 13:20-21

Catholic Bibles

Ignatius Bible, RSV

New American Bible

New Revised Standard Version Catholic Edition

Stay Connected

The following provide reliable sources for good Catholic reading, listening, viewing, book purchasing, and Bible purchasing. Find many sources available in several mediums. Some publications are available at church at no cost, indicated by asterisk.

AugustineInstitute.org

CatholicsComeHome.org

CatholicCompany.com

*Catholic Free Press**

CatholicFreePress.org

Catholictv.org

DynamicCatholic.com

EWTN.com (Eternal Word Television Network)

Ignatius.com

*Living Faith—Daily Catholic Devotions**

LivingFaith.com

LivingFaithKids.com

LoyolaPress.com

Magnificat.com

Marian.org (Assoc. of Marian Helpers)

PrayMoreNovenas.com

RachelsVineyard.org

Renewalministries.net

Thedivinemercy.org

WAU.com (Word Among Us)

About the Author

Kathleen Bennett

public domain photo by LifeTouch

Kathleen, called Kathy, Bennett is a returning Catholic since 2009. Her divergent paths brought her to her knees after thirty years of living in the void. Motivated by her own journey back to the loving and merciful arms of God, she recognized the inspiration of the Holy Spirit in her wish to write this book to share some of the richness that Catholicism encompasses.

Her devout parents gave her six years of parochial school at Sacred Heart Parish in Gardner, and she finished her religious education through the Sacrament of Confirmation in the Sacred Heart Parish CCD program.

Holy Cross Parish also offers the Rite of Christian Initiation of Adults, RCIA. To Kathy's delight, her husband, Gary, became fully initiated into the Church after they both attended RCIA sessions together in 2018.

Kathy is a parishioner of Holy Cross Parish, serving on its religious education board. She has two grown children in other parts of the state and is the grandmother of three.

Acknowledgments

Many special thanks to

- Father Patrick Ssekyole for his invaluable theological review and contributory editing and to Holy Cross Parish for enabling the publication of *Bounty Now and Forever*
- Richard Bruno for proofreading
- Christine Schroeder for diligent copy editing
- Haley's, the publisher, for expertise every step of the way for my first published body of work. Thank you, Marcia.

Colophon

Text for *Bounty Now and Forever* is set in Century Schoolbook, a transitional serif typeface designed by Morris Fuller Benton in 1919 for the American Type Founders at the request of Ginn & Co., a textbook publisher that wanted an especially easy-to-read face for textbooks. Century Schoolbook is based on the earlier Century Roman.

Century Schoolbook is familiar to many in North America as the typeface many first learned to read. Morris Fuller Benton utilized research done by Clark University that showed young readers more quickly identified letter-forms with contrasting weight but lighter strokes.

Titles and captions for *Bounty Now and Forever* are set in Franklin Gothic, a large family of realist sans-serif typefaces developed by the type foundry American Type Founders and credited to its head designer Morris Fuller Benton.

Franklin Gothic has been used in many advertisements and headlines in newspapers. The typeface appears in a variety of media from books to billboards.

www.ingramcontent.com/pod-product-compliance
Lightning Source LLC
Chambersburg PA
CBHW060403050426
42449CB00009B/1880

* 9 7 8 1 9 4 8 3 8 0 1 3 3 *